# Barker

**Story written by Gill Munton**
**Illustrated by Tim Archbold**

# Speed Sounds

**Consonants**   *Ask children to say the sounds.*

| f | l | m | n | r | s | v | z | sh | th | ng |
|---|---|---|---|---|---|---|---|----|----|----|
| ff | ll | mm | nn | rr | ss | ve | zz | | | nk |
| ph | le | mb | **kn** | wr | se | | se | | | |
| | | | | | ce | | s | | | |

| b | c | d | g | h | j | p | qu | t | w | x | y | ch |
|---|---|---|---|---|---|---|----|---|---|---|---|-----|
| bb | k | dd | gg | | g | pp | | tt | wh | | | **tch** |
| | ck | | | | **ge** | | | | | | | |

*Each box contains one sound but sometimes more than one grapheme.*
*Focus graphemes for this story are **circled**.*

## Vowels

*Ask children to say the sounds in and out of order.*

| a | e<br>ea | i | o | u | ay | ee<br>y<br>e | igh<br>i | ow<br>o |
|---|---|---|---|---|---|---|---|---|
| at | hen | in | on | up | day | see | high | blow |

| oo | oo | **ar** | or<br>oor<br>ore | air | ir | ou | oy<br>oi |
|---|---|---|---|---|---|---|---|
| zoo | look | car | for | fair | whirl | shout | boy |

# Story Green Words

*Ask children to read the words first in Fred Talk and then say the word.*

darts match   pinch   shelf   keen   chunk   arm   scar

guard dog*   grey*   paw*

---

*Ask children to say the syllables and then read the whole word.*

post|man   sand|wich|es   car|ton   car|toon   post|card

---

*Ask children to read the root first and then the whole word with the suffix.*

bark → barks   rip → ripped   knock → knocked

charge → charged   wash → washed*

*\* Challenge Words*

6

# Vocabulary Check

*Discuss the meaning (as used in the story) after the children have read each word.*

| | definition: | sentence: |
|---|---|---|
| **fed up** | cross with | They were all fed up with Barker. |
| **darts match** | throwing game | Grandad was at a darts match. |
| **pinch** | take | Then he started to pinch food. |
| **chunk** | bit | He was running away with a big chunk of beef. |
| **keen** | pleased or liked | Mum wasn't too keen on muddy paw marks. |
| **charged** | rushed | Barker charged up to him. |
| **guard dog** | a dog that protects people | Meet Barker the guard dog! |

# Red Words

*Ask children to practise reading the words across the rows, down the columns and in and out of order clearly and quickly.*

| does | were | all | one |
|------|------|-----|-----|
| said | of | to | they |
| were | some | any | was |
| want | are | where | you |
| your | watch | there | their |

# Barker

Barker's my dog.
He's the best!
He's big, dark grey and a bit smelly.
(He rolls in mud a lot.)

He barks a lot, too. In fact, he does lots of bad things.
Mum, Dad, Grandad and the postman were all fed up with Barker.

Until the day that ...

No, let's start at the beginning with Grandad's slippers.

Barker had lots of fun with them. One night,
when Grandad was at a darts match, Barker
got hold of one of the slippers
and ripped it apart!

Grandad said, "No, Barker."
And Barker just barked.

Then he started to pinch food from the kitchen. Jam tarts,
cheese sandwiches and jelly. Barker wasn't fussy.

Mum left a dish of cold beef on a shelf, and Barker
jumped up to get it. A carton of milk, a jar of plum jam –
Barker knocked them off the shelf to get to the beef.

He looked like a cartoon dog, running away
from Mum with a big chunk of beef
between his teeth!

Mum said, "No, Barker."
And Barker just barked.

Oh, yes, and Mum wasn't too keen on the muddy paw marks. When Barker slept on my bed one night, the sheets had to be washed the next day!

I said, "No, Barker."

And Barker just barked.

We had a bad day when Barker bit the postman. He was bringing us a postcard from Dad's pal Mark (on holiday in Cardiff).

Barker charged up to him and bit his arm.
(He's got sharp teeth, my dog.
The postman's still got the scar.)

The postman said, "No, Barker."
And Barker just barked.

The next day, Barker was sick in the car, at Farnham car park. Barker grabbed an old hotdog from a bin, and when we got back to the car he looked a bit ill. We all got in, and as soon as Dad started up the car, Barker was sick ...

very sick indeed.

And we were still in the car park!

Dad said "No Barker."

And Barker just barked.

Then, one night, he started
barking when we were all asleep in bed!

Dad went to see what was up.
The kitchen window was smashed, and
Dad spotted some men running away
from the flat!

"Meet Barker the guard dog!" I said.
"Smart dog, Barker! You're a star!"

That night, they all agreed with me.

# Questions to talk about

*Ask children to TTYP each question using 'Fastest finger' (FF) or 'Have a think' (HaT).*

**p.9** (FF)  Who was fed up with Barker?

**p.10** (FF)  What did Barker do when Grandad was at a darts match?

**p.11** (FF)  What did Barker do when Mum told him off?

**p.12** (HaT)  Why do you think Mum didn't want Barker going on the bed?

**p.13** (FF)  What did Barker do to the postman?

**p.14** (FF)  What made Barker sick?

**p.15** (HaT)  Who were the men who were running away?

# Questions to read and answer

*(Children complete without your help.)*

1. What did Barker do with Grandad's slipper?
**He ripped it apart. / He hid it. / He licked it.**

2. What did Barker pinch from the kitchen?
**He pinched drinks from the kitchen. / He pinched food from the kitchen. / He pinched slippers from the kitchen.**

3. Where did Barker bite the postman?
**Barker bit the postman on the arm. / Barker bit the postman on the leg.**

4. What did Barker do in the car?
**Barker slept in the car. / Barker hid in the car. / Barker was sick in the car.**

5. What did Dad say to Barker in the end?
**You are a sad dog. / You are a smart dog. / You are a bad dog.**

# Speedy Green Words

*Ask children to practise reading the words across the rows, down the columns and in and out of order clearly and quickly.*

| | | | |
|---|---|---|---|
| until | beginning | apart | between |
| indeed | agreed | best | things |
| night | just | started | food |
| slept | next | night | asleep |
| kitchen | away | running | smart |